T0209946

SEX, DRUGS & *THE LOVE OF* GOD

ELLEN HARLOW

WestBow
PRESS®
A DIVISION OF THOMAS NELSON
& ZONDERVAN

WestBow Press books may be ordered through booksellers or by contacting:

WestBow Press
A Division of Thomas Nelson & Zondervan
1663 Liberty Drive
Bloomington, IN 47403
www.westbowpress.com
844-714-3454

All scripture quotations are taken from the Holy Bible, New International Version, copyright (c) 1973, 1978, 1984, 2011 by Biblica, Inc. Used by permission. All rights reserved worldwide.

ISBN: 979-8-3850-0913-8 (sc)
ISBN: 979-8-3850-0914-5 (hc)
ISBN: 979-8-3850-0915-2 (e)

Library of Congress Control Number: 2023918995

Print information available on the last page.

WestBow Press rev. date: 01/10/2024

ACKNOWLEDGMENTS

Many hands have thumbed through the pages of this book.

Tina Burden, Pat Miesner, Cindy Sanes, and Amy Wilkinson, with your time and effort given to editing and providing constructive feedback, I will be forever grateful to each of you! I love you dearly!

To the reader, may the Holy Spirit fill your heart to overflowing as you journey through the pages of this book.

Last and most importantly, thank you, Jesus, for letting me know thirty-one years ago I would be writing a book; although, at the time, I really thought You might be kidding because I hate to read. It is now obvious You were extremely serious. It is the desire of my heart that this book will change lives for Your Glory and Yours alone.

FOREWORD

My introduction to Ellen Harlow was through the Bible Application Class, an interdenominational Bible study for men and women, taught by the founder of the class Cheryl Hall. Ellen and I were in the same small group, and these women became the body of Christ to one another. That period in Ellen's life could be described as "sweet, salty, and sour!" The words sweet and salty refer to the bond of Christ's love that connected our members and ministered to those who were in need. The word sour applied to her difficult living situation at that time. Her small rented cinderblock house was as cold as a vacant castle! But that was where we brought groceries to her when money was short! Our first year together in BAC was one of spiritual growth, both as individuals and as a caring little church family.

Ellen's story is evidence of the powerful work of our mighty God! Ellen had a deep hole in her heart from the wounds of her childhood and youth. But our gracious Lord filled that empty cavity and turned it into a wellspring of rejoicing and thanksgiving. God pursued Ellen—His precious, lost child—and brought her back home to Himself. Loving His children is what God does best! He can be as gentle or tenacious as needed, but He is relentless when it comes to His flock.

Lose one of His own? Never!

Just ask Ellen.

John 18:9

Louise Wells

CONTENTS

INTRODUCTION: SEX, DRUGS, AND THE LOVE OF GOD

The book you're about to read is God's hand at work in a real, clear, and undeniable way. The collection of stories here is true; and although names have been changed to protect the privacy of the parties involved, the one name above all names is still the same—that is, Jesus Christ, Son of the Living God!

I believe our Lord and Savior will work through all who read this book. While some will be drawn closer to Him, others will meet Him for the first time and seeds will be planted.

You'll find the Holy Spirit in action, along with God's truth, mercy, and abounding grace woven throughout each story. May our Lord and Savior Christ Jesus touch your heart and guide your thoughts and emotions as you encounter His awesome power, great simplicity, and, most of all, His amazing love. Enjoy and be encouraged as you experience hope, healing, and transformation to be the person He created you to be.

PRAISE THE LORD FOR BEING MY EVERYTHING

I'm Ellen Harlow, and the Lord is the very essence of my being. I can't do anything without Him because I know I'm not capable of making decisions, much less carrying them out, without His direction. This has been proven time and again in my life, and, by George, I believe I've finally got it!

Like so many folks, I was raised in a good ole Baptist environment. I accepted Jesus in my heart as my Lord and Savior at the age of twelve, and I was baptized shortly thereafter. I can remember my heart being so full of hope and promise as the tears saturated my face. I was so relieved to know I would spend eternity with Jesus in heaven and not in hell with Satan and his angels. Those were the days when amen was said out loud and "Praise the Lord" was heard every time someone felt blessed. Now, you hardly ever hear amen, not to mention "Praise the Lord!" I'm not just talking about the Baptists. This applies to many other denominations.

You see, my life has been full of deceit, dishonesty, and lies that revolved around unspeakable secrets. I was sexually abused until the age of ten by a some adults in my life. I'm not exactly sure when it all began, although I do remember some things as far back as the crib. I remember being told that I couldn't tell anyone because my parents would get angry and wouldn't love me anymore. I was also told no one would ever believe me. If I'd only known then that it wasn't my fault as my body had betrayed me.

This wasn't hard for me to believe since my parents showed very little affection toward me. In fact, my mother nearly died when she gave birth to me. I can't remember her ever holding or kissing me. My father was the only one who let me hug and kiss him, even though he never initiated it. My mom never cared for hugging. She said it was mushy stuff, and she didn't like it.

I depended on my dad—I was his little girl. He stuck up for me when my mom spanked me, as I never seemed to do anything right in her eyes. Although he defended me, the spanking never stopped, but it just helped me to know someone cared about me.

My mom wore the pants in our family. My dad had no education—but, boy, he had common sense! As unusual as it sounds, he could add, subtract, and multiply in his head in seconds. That always amazed me! My mom, on the other hand, had a ninth-grade education. She was the one who managed the bills and made sure everything was properly handled.

In 1973, when I was nineteen, we found out my dad was dying. I felt like I was in a dream and I'd wake up any moment, but unfortunately, it didn't happen. The doctors gave him about six to twelve months to live. They said the cancer had spread beyond treatment, and they couldn't do anything for him.

In March 1974, we received word that my grandfather had killed himself. That was always debatable, but my mother went back home to help her sisters make all the necessary arrangements while I stayed at our place to look after my dad. It was a scary time for me because Dad got real bad after Mom left. I took him to the hospital. Mom traveled back and forth until her father was buried. Then arrived the time we all dreaded. It had only been a couple of weeks since my grandfather had died, and now my mom had to deal with the imminent death of her husband.

I remember that night as though it were yesterday. Dad went into a coma right after he kissed me and told me he loved me. I was in shock as I lay there beside him, holding his hand, waiting for my mom and brother to return to the hospital. You know, back then, when someone was dying, the entire neighborhood would show up! As I lay on the bed beside him, I heard one of the little old ladies from the community say, "Why, he could lie there for days like that!"

When I heard that, I said, "Dear Lord, please don't let my daddy lie here and suffer."

It was at that moment this little voice (the Holy Spirit) said, "Sit up and look at your daddy." When I did, I watched him easily release his last breath. I couldn't believe what I'd just seen. I left the hospital that night in a daze. As I drove home, I remember listening to Jim Croce singing "Time in a Bottle." It's funny how things like that stick with you.

After the funeral, I really got mad at God! I couldn't believe how He'd left me with a hateful old woman like my mother. I walked away from Him. I worked a full-time job, so getting back to work was good for me. The one thing I didn't plan on was being seduced by a woman who was old enough to be my mother. She loved me like no one else did. It was new and exciting, and in some ways, it was comforting. This went on for about a year after my dad's death. I became restless and decided to leave home and get out on my own.

I thought moving away would help get my life together. Somehow, I would find the peace, love, and acceptance I longed for. As soon as I'd moved and settled, an old friend from high school showed up and wanted to take me out and show me around the big city. Little did I know I would find myself in gay nightclubs, drinking and smoking cigarettes and marijuana. This led to cocaine, acid, and all kinds of other drugs. I was so lost within myself.

I spent twenty years of my life in several relationships with women, partying, singing in gay nightclubs, and continuing in the drug scene. I was a mess! I just couldn't seem to get it together. In homosexual relationships, you move one partner out while bringing another one in. Homosexuals have very little downtime between partners. Many may want to jump on the bandwagon and debate it. Yes, there are exceptions, but in no way is there a justifiable exception.

I remember one night in particular when I spoke to the Lord for the first time in twenty years. I said, "Lord, I am so tired of this life, but I can't get out of it by myself!" I told Him if He were really there, He would have to get me out of this relationship because I wasn't capable of doing it on my own.

It was about a year after that when the woman I lived with told me she was leaving. I was crushed because I was always the one who left—I always had someone waiting to take their place. This time, I was being left alone, and I had no one waiting to do anything! I was alone for the first time in my life since my dad's death. Again, I heard that little voice (the Holy Spirit) say, "You asked for this."

I couldn't help but think, *Yes, I asked for this a year ago but not now!* This was my first experience with the Lord's timing and not mine. I cried out to Jesus. I fell on my knees in the middle of the living room floor and screamed at the Lord. I shouted out to Him, "If my lifestyle is really wrong, then You show me! You let me know that it's wrong! You can show me in Your Word [the Holy Bible]." I jumped up from the middle of that living room floor and started to search for my paperback copy of *The Living Bible*, the one I'd received from a Billy Graham crusade when I was a young girl. I could hardly see because of all the tears while searching box after box for that Bible.

I finally found it, and I said, "Lord, since You are God and You can do anything, You can show me if I'm living wrong. I'm just going to get in bed, and You'll have to make sure I open it and start reading where I'm supposed to start reading because I have no idea where to look!" I got all situated in bed and propped my head up on one arm. I opened the Bible and started to read. This is what I read:

> Don't you know that those doing such things have no share in the Kingdom of God? Don't fool yourselves. Those who live immoral lives, who

are idol worshipers, adulterers or homosexuals—
will have no share in his kingdom (1 Corinthians
6:9–10).

I flew straight up out of that bed and briskly walked through
that house, crying, praising, and thanking Christ Jesus for answering
me. I know that if anyone had been outside my house, they would've
thought I'd lost my mind! That night, I slept like a baby.

The next morning, on the way into work, I was on cloud nine
until this little voice said, "Huh . . you know that was that old
Billy Graham translation, and you know you've always heard that
the King James Version was the most accurate translation." All of
a sudden, my balloon was busted! I was deflated for the entire day!

When I got home, I hurried inside because I remembered I
had a huge family Bible I'd found in a vacant apartment that was
packed away in another box. I thought it might be a King James,
and sure enough, it was. I quickly opened it and read the passage,
and the word *homosexual* wasn't mentioned anywhere. I was right
back where I started.

I fell back down on my knees and began to cry and pleaded with
Jesus to please help me. I said, "Lord, I've always heard that we aren't
supposed to question You, but if You'll show me one more time, I
promise I'll never ask You again! Please just show me like you did
last night." I jumped up and grabbed that same Billy Graham Bible,
not realizing that this translation was the reason I asked Him to
show me again in the first place. I jumped into bed as if to reenact
exactly what occurred the night before. I said, "Lord, I'm just going
to open it up, so please direct my eyes just like you did last night."
This is what I read:

> That is why God let go of them and let them do
> all these evil things, so that even their women
> turned against God's natural plan for them and
> indulged in sex sin with each other. And the men,

instead of having a normal sex relationship with women, burned with lust for each other, men doing shameful things with other men and as a result, getting paid within their own souls with the penalty they so richly deserved (Romans 1:26–27).

This time, I bolted straight up out of that bed and hit my knees crying, thanking, and praising Him with all my heart and soul. No speed walking through the house this time. I knew he was there! Then, this small little voice (the Holy Spirit) said, "Stand up, go, and look in the King James." Needless to say, it said the very same thing; and to this day, my life has never been the same!

Jesus has directed my life ever since that day in 1992. I promised Him that night I would give myself to Him for His mighty work. I prayed and asked him for several things that night to bring praise and glory to His name.

#1: "Lord, please allow me to continue to sing and write songs. I promise I will do it all for your glory and not for my personal gain."

#2: "Lord, please clean up my nasty mouth." Every other word that came out of my mouth was trash.

#3: "I give myself to you for a mighty work that will bring praise and glory to your name. Lord, I will tell everyone what you have done for me, but you know that I can't do it while my mama is still alive."

#4: "Lord, please don't let my mama ever die and leave me with any guilt or regret because, Lord, you know I could not live with myself."

My first request was immediately answered. I wrote two songs and recorded them. My second request was answered a few days later. In fact, it shocked me so badly because the word I was about to say was not the word that flew out of my mouth! Bad language ended that day! Not that I haven't slipped up since that day, but I can assure you, it's not a common occurrence, and I'm quick to ask my Lord to forgive me.

My third request unexpectedly came a few years later. My recording studio approached me about taking a poem someone wrote and putting it into music. When I finished rewriting the words and adding the music, I was so touched I paid to record it myself. It was a song titled "Memories and Times." It was a song about the death of a mother that I made my own. I took it home, and Mom and I listened to it in her car. After it finished playing, she affectionately punched me on the leg and said, "See there, that's the way it is. You don't miss us till we're gone." We laughed.

I had no idea that one year later this song would begin to play out in its entirety. It was Thanksgiving Day, and as always, I went home to take Mom out to eat. I knew she went to the doctor, and the doctor wanted me to call him when I arrived. When she opened the door for me, I knew something was terribly wrong! I tried not to show my concern because I didn't want to worry her.

I had to help her into a vehicle for the first time in my life and help her out when we arrived at the restaurant. I had to fix her plate also, which is something I never had to do. She hardly ate anything. I tried to encourage her and say things, like, "Oh, the doctor just wanted to tell me that you need some help at home or something like that."

We left the restaurant. I drove over to the hospital and went inside while Mom waited in the truck. They paged the doctor and told me he would call back in just a minute. He did. When I answered the phone and heard him tell me that my mom was going to die, a part of me died that very moment. He gave her about six months to live, and I was devastated.

The Lord was in total control. He was answering my fourth prayer request to fulfill my third prayer request. My job gave me a leave of absence. I was able to come home and take care of my mom. For the first time in my entire life, we were able to talk and tell each other how much we loved one another. She told me how proud she was of me, how my life had changed, and how thankful she was that the Lord allowed her to see it. I had the chance to tell her how proud

I was to have her as my mom and how much I appreciated her raising me to know the Lord even though I strayed for a time. We also had the chance to talk about her seeing the Lord, seeing Daddy and her mom, etc. Most importantly, we prayed together, asking the Lord not to let her suffer but to take her home to be with Him.

The Lord allowed me to be with my mom from Thanksgiving Day 1997 through January 13, 1998. He allowed me to hold her hand when she drew her last breath. What a Mighty God we serve! Last but not least, the song "Memories and Times" played out in its entirety—every lyric and every emotion, even down to the weather outside. Jesus knew from beginning to end, for perfection is His entire being. Won't you let Him direct your life from beginning to end? I assure you that He's the only one who can turn what seems to be an impossible situation into a possible one, sadness into joy, and confusion into peace. If you haven't yielded your life to Christ, please don't let this moment pass you by because you may never have another opportunity. He stands knocking if only you will answer. If you're reading this and desire to speak with me about overcoming your past, no matter the sin(s) involved, please feel free to contact me via my website: www.HeartofJesusMinistries.com.

BAD-HABIT DELIVERANCE

When my life changed, it was a gradual thing. Believe me, all my bad habits didn't leave at once. In fact, it took a little over five years to be rid of one of them completely. I had a few people who remained a social aspect of my life after I asked Jesus to come into my heart. In the beginning, I was always going over to one of their homes because I knew I could catch a marijuana buzz. This seemed to be the hardest thing for me to give up. I guess you could say I was a "pothead." The Lord had taken away the homosexual lifestyle, the drinking, hard drugs, the cigarettes, and a foul mouth; but marijuana was something I just couldn't seem to turn away from.

I prayed and prayed as time went on about jumping every time I had an offer to catch a buzz from anyone. I could go for weeks without a buzz, but let me get a call; and once again, I found myself getting high. I justified it by saying, "Well, the Lord understands. I don't do it that often." It seemed the more I made excuses, the more convinced I'd be that my actions were acceptable. There were those who would always say, "Oh, Ellen, you have overcome so much, and I don't think the Lord minds if you get high once in a while. After all, He made it, and you deserve it! It's not like you're out barhopping or something like that!"

This continued for about six years until one day I started crying. I had gotten my buzz, and I was on my way back home. I was so convicted about subjecting the Holy Spirit of the Lord that dwelled inside me to this behavior. I cried out to Him, saying, "Lord, I can't stop this by myself. Please help me!"

A few weeks passed when I received a phone call. I was invited to come over, get a buzz (to get high on marijuana), and join the cookout. I went driving down the road, headed for that buzz (a feeling of being high on marijuana). I said, "Lord, please help me to reject the offer to get high. Please, Lord, I can't do it alone." People were standing everywhere I sat in the living room—high as a kite, waiting to eat—when, all of a sudden, I experienced the most frightening, unwelcome feeling in their home. It was an awful feeling of evil despair. I finally got up and told them I couldn't stay for the cookout, and I left in tears.

As I drove home, I heard this little voice (the Holy Spirit) saying, "I bet you'll stay away from there now." At that moment, I started telling the Lord how I knew He was in control of this. Between the tears, I began to praise Him and thank Him.

I'm truly blessed. To this day, I haven't smoked any marijuana. I realized the Lord allowed this to happen when He did because He knew it would take something of this magnitude to turn me away. Let's face it, I don't know very many people who can have an experience like this and still want to go back and run the risk of having another frightening experience like that, do you?

> "Therefore, come out from them and be separate," says the Lord. "Touch no unclean thing and I will receive you." "I will be a Father to you, and you will be my sons and daughters, says the Lord Almighty" (2 Corinthians 6:17–18).

LESSONS FROM THE PRAYING MANTIS

There was a situation in my life that always seemed to keep my nerves on edge. It involved those who always tried to tell me what to do with my money. Not that there's anything wrong with someone giving you advice, but it just seemed they always delivered their advice as if I were incompetent to manage my finances. They always tried to tell me what to do with my money, which was on a scale of 2 compared to their scale of 100. I cried out to the Lord one night and asked Him to please let me know how to handle this situation.

The next day after work, I left my office to take the company mail to the mailbox. I started to drop the mail in the slot when I was startled by a large six-inch praying mantis sitting on the edge of the box. I snatched my hand back because it startled me. After realizing what it was, I said, "So are you making sure everyone puts their mail in?" I laughed and drove away.

The next morning, I got into my truck to go to work; and as I started to shut the door, I was startled to see another large six-inch praying mantis on my door. I backed out of the driveway, hoping he'd jump off, but he didn't. I stopped and slid an envelope under him and put him over in the grass by my mailbox. I said, "Have a good day." I could hardly wait to get to work so I could tell the girls I worked with what happened the night before and that morning. I even wondered if it might be the same praying mantis I saw in the company mailbox, but I couldn't figure out how he could ride on my truck for over fifteen miles and not blow off.

That night, when I went to bed, I prayed regarding the situation in my life that kept my nerves torn apart. I finished my prayers, turned on my radio (which I listen to all night long while I sleep), and got into bed. As I was settling in for the night, a program came on the radio called *Creation Moments*. They said they were going to talk about one of the most intelligent insects in the world. I became real still because I thought to myself, *If they say praying mantis, I'm gonna lose it*. Well, you guessed it, it was the Praying Mantis. They said they were so smart. If anyone gave them something to eat and it made them sick, they would never touch anything again that even resembled the substance that made them sick.

The moral I received from this story was when something keeps you all torn up inside, leave it alone—get away from it.

Was it a coincidence I had an encounter with a praying mantis two days in a row and then hear about it on the radio that night? I don't think so! We serve an awesome God who will answer if only we believe and ask with expectancy.

> I call on you, Oh God, for you will answer me; give
> ear to me and hear my prayer (Psalm 17:6).

MY SHEEP, LISTEN!

I arrived at work one morning, and what a busy morning it was. At the time, I worked for a construction office that installed cabling for private residences as well as large corporations. I had a lot of data entry that morning, and I also had to get all the deposits for the company ready to go to the bank before 2:00 p.m. I sat down at my desk and started working. Before I knew it, it was noon.

I stretched my arms back and released a big yawn. I was sitting at the desk since eight that morning, and I really needed to get up and walk around a bit, but I didn't. I continued to prepare all the bank deposits so that when I got up from my desk, I could put them all in the appropriate envelopes on the wall behind me.

After I completed everything, I got up from my desk and put the deposit slips in the envelopes on the wall. After I finished, I turned to sit back down when, all of a sudden, I heard this still, small voice (the Holy Spirit) say, "Don't sit down."

I thought to myself, *Why am I hearing that?*

I moved my chair back to sit down when I heard once again, "Don't sit down. Look under your desk."

By this time, I was a little uneasy (to say the least). All I know is that I moved my chair and got down on my hands and knees. I looked up under my desk, which was dark because it was in the corner of my office.

I saw something, but I couldn't make out what it was. I thought, *Now, you know that's not a snake, right?* I reached into my drawer, pulled out a ruler, reached out, and touched it. All of a sudden, it struck me, sending me flying back against the wall in shock!

I slowly got up off the floor and walked over to the stairwell. Everyone already went to lunch except for one guy upstairs and me. I called up to him and said very calmly, "Can you come down here? There's a snake under my desk!"

He yelled back down and said, "You're kidding me!"

I said, "No, there really is! Hurry up!"

He flew down the stairs and slowly walked into my office. He peeked under my desk and said, "You're right. I can't believe this."

He told me to stay there and watch to make sure the snake didn't come out of my office until he could get back with a box and pipe to catch it.

He caught the snake, which turned out to be a baby copperhead. While this snake is not known for causing many deaths in the United States, it has, however, caused people to die by their bite. I was really glad I didn't know all this before I got down on my hands and knees looking under that desk! Ha! Nonetheless, I know the Lord was looking out for me, and I thank Him from the bottom of my heart. I'm extremely blessed!

> Jesus answered, "I told you, but you don't believe. Everything I have done has been authorized by my Father, actions that speak louder than words. You don't believe because you're not my sheep. My sheep recognize my voice. I know them, and they follow me. I give them real and eternal life. They are protected from the Destroyer for good. No one can steal them from out of my hand. The Father who put them under my care is so much greater than the Destroyer and Thief. No one could ever get them away from him. I and the Father are one heart and mind" (John 10:27–28, The Message).

OBEYING THE HOLY SPIRIT

One afternoon, after I got home from work, I practiced some songs I planned to sing for the local Veteran's Administration Hospital to entertain the patients on Because We Care Day. After I finished practicing, I started to watch television. I also started talking with the Lord. I often talk with the Lord on and off during the day no matter where I am or what I may be doing. For me, this isn't unusual.

On this particular day, I was flipping through the channels on the television when I asked the Lord what He wanted me to do for Him. I was led by the Holy Spirit to stop on a channel that was showing a big brick building. It was an orphanage. The man being interviewed explained how there was no heat in the building and that it was the dead of winter. They were praying and depending on the Lord to help them with a solution. I continued to watch the program.

The story continued as the man gave praise and glory to Jesus for the following day was so beautiful that they were able to let all the children in the orphanage go outside and play in the warmth of the sunshine. At that moment, I felt the Holy Spirit leading me to call an orphanage located in the area where I lived and make an appointment to go and see them.

As I prayed that night, I told the Lord I would call Information the next morning and inquire as to where I could locate an orphanage in the area. The next morning, I inquired about orphanages in the area, and the operator told me two orphanages were located in a little town approximately an hour or so away from where I lived. The Holy Spirit led me to call The Central Children's Home. I called and made an appointment with the director. I told him I'd like to come and talk with him. On the day of my appointment, I left work early and headed to the orphanage.

As I entered the outskirts of the town, I looked for the name of the street where the director told me to turn to find the orphanage. As soon as I turned onto the street, I saw the sign for The Central Children's Home. I pulled into the parking lot and noticed quite a few people standing outside. I realized this was an African American orphanage.

When I walked into the building, everyone appeared to be watching me. The director greeted me with a firm handshake. He grinned as if to say, "What in the world can this white woman do for my orphanage?" You can just imagine how I stood out like a sore thumb: white girl, blonde hair, blue eyes—well, you get the picture!

We entered his office, and he said, "Well, Ellen, what can I do for you?"

I said, "First of all, I must be honest with you. I really don't know why I'm here. I only know that the Lord led me here. I don't know what, or if, I can help here in any way."

The director proceeded to share with me a bit of history about the orphanage and told me about several children who lived there. He also gave me a book about the orphanage. It was a good experience for me. Finally, he said, "Ellen, we only have one position open here at the school, and we've offered it to a young lady, and we're waiting for her answer as to whether she's going to accept the offer. I'm not sure you'd have any experience or interest in this area, but the opening is for a music director."

I started grinning! I reached into my purse and pulled out one of my demo tapes and handed it to him. He started grinning. He told me he would definitely give me a call if the lady whom they offered the position didn't accept it.

In the end, the orphanage never called me back. My visit to the orphanage was wonderful and educational. I left there that day and cried tears of joy all the way home. As I drove home, I thanked and praised the Lord for leading me there. All of a sudden, I heard these words, "Sometimes the Holy Spirit will lead us to do things that appear for nothing just because the Lord wants to see if we will be obedient." Until that moment, I never thought so deeply about things that I've been led to do in the past. I know now that when I'm being led to do something, I'm much more attentive and aware of the presence of the Holy Spirit.

That day, I realized the importance of being obedient and sensitive to the Lord, His voice, and His guidance. It's so easy sometimes when I feel led to do something to just chalk it up to my desires instead of stopping to test the spirits to ensure it's of my Lord and Savior Jesus Christ and not some evil spirit of deception that desires to harm me and lead me astray.

The realization and understanding of the power that dwells within me must be obeyed, or I could face the consequences resulting from my disobedience. I've learned that obeying the voice of my Lord is much more important than anything I can ever do in my human nature. In fact, it's a necessity.

> If you ever forget the LORD your God and follow other gods and worship and bow down to them, I testify against you today that you will surely be destroyed. Like the nations the LORD destroyed before you, so you will be destroyed for not obeying the LORD your God (Deuteronomy 8:19–20).

> But Samuel replied: "Does the LORD delight in burnt offerings and sacrifices as much as in obeying the voice of the LORD? To obey is better than sacrifice, and to heed is better than the fat of rams" (1 Samuel 15:22).

WARFARE IS REAL

One day, just before I got off work, I returned my mother's telephone call. She always had a way of ruffling my feathers. She always—or, rather, I always allowed her to put me on guilt trips over the smallest things. This was my insecurity and weakness where my mother was concerned.

This particular day, after I hung up the phone, I was in tears. At this time, I was a new student of the Word of God (the Bible), and there were things I still didn't understand yet. As I walked to my truck to leave work, with tears streaming down my face, I said, "Lord, please help me."

I got in my truck and headed down the highway, crying as I listened to the message on the gospel radio station. I chimed in with the preacher on the radio as he said, "The Lord will send you a comforter."

I said, "Yes, Lord, I know you will send me a comforter, and I'll be all right."

Little did I realize I was already filled with the comforter, the Holy Spirit, that God has promised to come inside each believer: "And I will ask the Father, and he will give you another Counselor to be with you forever" (John 14:16).

I came to a stoplight. I was praising the Lord and seeking His comfort and peace when this man in my rearview mirror got my attention. He didn't say anything—he didn't even look at me. He was just sitting in his van, staring up at the sky with such an angelic look. All of a sudden, I felt the presence of the Lord, and I spoke out, saying, "Thank you, Lord, for making your presence known to me. I know it's you."

No sooner had I gotten that out of my mouth did I hear this sultry voice saying, "But is it?"

It sent chills down my back, and I felt such fear like I'd never felt before in my life. Everything seemed to happen simultaneously. I heard the voice, the light changed, and I had to turn. As I was turning, my radio station shot across the dial to a heavy-metal station. It scared me silly! I couldn't get that station back on the gospel station quickly enough!

Then I started praising the Lord and rebuking the devil. I felt the warfare so heavy, and I knew my radio station couldn't have been changed by accidentally hitting the button. It had no buttons! To change the dial, you had to turn the knob and hold it too!

I realized what had happened after I got home. My walk with the Lord was just beginning, as was my warfare with the powers of the air. Before, I was an enemy of God and on Satan's side; now, I was an enemy of Satan and on God's side! It was better to be on God's side!

I'm not sure if what I saw in my rearview mirror that day was really there, and I'll probably never know for sure in this life. However, I do know the Lord has a mighty work for me to do for Him, and this was the beginning of many encounters to come. The devil uses our insecurities and weaknesses to trip us up, so we'll stay in the "old familiar life" that's controlled by him and not give ourselves totally to the Lord.

I thank you, Lord, for always being there for me when I call on you. I thank you for allowing me to serve You and bring praise and glory to Your name. Amen!

> The thief comes only to steal and kill and destroy; I have come that they may have life, and have it to the full. I am the good shepherd. The good shepherd lays down his life for the sheep (John 10:9–11).

WHEN GOD SPEAKS, LISTEN AND OBEY!

It was early one morning when I was getting dressed for work that I heard the Holy Spirit speak to me, saying, "You need to talk to Gary today."

I stopped dead still in the middle of dressing and started to chuckle, saying, "Lord, I just don't know about that."

Gary is a homosexual man who works at my office, and he's very open about his homosexuality. He's also very young; in fact, he could be my son if I had one. I could hardly stand to be around him. I've actually gone out of my way to avoid coming in contact with him.

I finished dressing and headed to work. I arrived, and as I swiped my badge to enter, the door wouldn't open. This never happened to me before. I always arrive at work early every morning, so it wasn't unusual that no one was there yet. As soon as I turned around to go back to my vehicle, a truck pulled up right next to mine. Guess who it was? It was Gary!

In my mind, I said, *Oh, Lord, I can't believe this!*

Then, the Holy Spirit said, "Go talk to him. Ask him if he's read any of your stories."

Well, I really didn't want to look at him, let alone talk with him, but I knew I had to be obedient to the Holy Spirit. After telling him that we couldn't get in the building, I said, "Hey, Gary, tell me something. Have you read any of my stories floating around the office?"

He said, "No, I haven't, but I would really like to read them." Then he added, "When we get in the building, don't forget to bring some of them to me."

I said, "All right." Just as I said that, someone opened the door. Imagine that! Ha!

I carried one of my stories over to him, and it wasn't long before he quickly came back over to my office with tears in his eyes. He said, "Ellen, you will never know what this story has done for me. I've felt just like you described your feelings in your story, the part that said you felt weighed down with fear." Then he added, "I've felt like that all my life. I see you here at work, and you're always talking about the Lord to everyone, and you always seem so happy. I really feel that I can talk to you."

Gary continued, "Do you think we could possibly go to lunch one day?"

I told him, "No." I said, "You're right. We do need to talk but not during lunch because I don't feel like an hour will be enough time to really talk. How about letting me take you to dinner one evening after work when we won't have any time clocks to punch?"

He agreed. I shared about Jesus with Gary and answered all his questions.

We both shed tears. I don't know if he's still in the homosexual lifestyle or not because he's taken a new job outside of my department. But I do know he does know the truth. I continue to pray for Gary, and I know in my heart the Lord orchestrated His will through me. We serve a most powerful, awesome God! What a Savior!

> He who obeys instructions guards his life, but he who is contemptuous of his ways will die (Proverbs 19:16).

IGNORING THE HOLY SPIRIT

On New Year's Day, I decided to go to a movie that night. It looked like it would be a good movie, so I got in my truck and headed that way. I got to the theater, bought my ticket, got a bottle of water, and found a good seat. The movie began when, all of a sudden, they spoke the Lord's name in vain. I cringed!

I was convinced with the thought that I should get up, ask for my money back, and leave. I justified staying by telling myself maybe it wouldn't happen again. In the middle of the movie, it was said again.

This time, I felt sick to my stomach while hearing in my spirit that I should get up and leave. Yet again, I justified staying by telling myself, *What good will it do for me to leave now? After all, no one would know why I was leaving but me.* So I continued to sit there and watch the movie.

Just before the end of the movie, it was said once again. My heart was really burdened to leave at that moment, but I justified staying one more time because I wanted to see the outcome of the movie.

After the movie ended, I headed to my truck. I felt so dirty. I started to cry, asking the Lord to please forgive me. I said, "Lord, I know you must be really disappointed in me. I should've just stayed home!"

I was so distraught. When I got home, I got down on my knees, prayed for forgiveness, and went to bed. The next morning, I left for work at six thirty in the dark. As I drove down that dark road, all of a sudden, what happened the night before came flooding through my mind once again. I started to cry and talked to Jesus again.

I couldn't apologize enough when, all of a sudden, the following thoughts flooded my heart and mind. As clear as a bell, He showed me exactly what I'd done. I acted just like Peter. I sat there and denied Him three times in a row. By denying Him, I quenched His Spirit that was telling me to get up and leave. Also, I might have prevented someone in that ticket booth from being aware that taking the Lord's name in vain is wrong. I should've gotten up in the beginning and asked for my money back.

When I got to work, I started telling people about what I'd done and what the Lord revealed to me. It wasn't until I shared this with someone that I felt peace within. I continue to share this to bring praise and glory to Jesus because He is truly in control of everything, including me. I can't praise and thank Him enough!

> Trust in the LORD with all your heart; do not depend on your own understanding. Seek His will in all you do, and He will direct your paths. Don't be impressed with your own wisdom. Instead, fear the LORD and turn your back on evil (Proverbs 3:5–7).

GOD KNOWS EVERYTHING FROM BEGINNING TO END

I was invited to sing and give my testimony at a church one Sunday night. I accepted the invitation and really felt blessed to have been asked. I prayed about what songs the Lord would have me sing, and as they were laid upon my heart, I began to practice them. I've always asked the Lord to direct me in the songs I sing, as well as the words He desires I speak, especially when I represent Him on these occasions.

Finally, that Sunday night arrived. I got my music together and loaded my equipment into my truck. I felt overwhelmed with the feeling I shouldn't sing one of the songs that I thought I'd been led to sing. I started to panic because there wasn't enough time to find another song. The thought was so powerful. It was impressed on me that I shouldn't sing the song I wrote about my mom dying because it would only depress folks. I should lift them up, not depress them. I was distraught because I didn't have enough time to change the music. I walked out the door and said, "Lord, please help me!" I immediately had a feeling that everything would be all right.

I entered the church building, and the service began. I became so nervous my hands started to sweat, and my mouth became dry. I felt extremely anxious. I called upon the Lord to help me again.

All of a sudden, I felt God's peace sweep over me just before they introduced me to give a testimony and sing.

I took my place in front of this congregation and began to speak. I'm always amazed at what comes out of my mouth because I realized a long time ago what I say can't be rehearsed. It must be led by the Holy Spirit.

The time came to sing the song I'd written about the death of my mother. I began to tell about how the Lord knows everything from beginning to end concerning what will happen in our lives. I explained how He gave me this song about my mother in the summer of 1996 and how every lyric in the song started to be fulfilled on Thanksgiving Day of 1997. It then concluded on January 13, 1998—the day Jesus took my mother home to be with Him.

After the service ended, I saw a young girl about twelve years old walking down the middle aisle straight toward me. With tears in her eyes, she stood in front of me with her trembling little voice and said, "That song about your mama dying meant so much to me. You see, my daddy died on January 13, 1997."

I just put my arms around her and hugged her. Tears fell from my eyes when suddenly a woman with tears in her eyes approached me from my left, saying, "I really needed to hear that song about your mama because, you see, I lost my mama on January 13 five years ago."

Not soon after she got those words out of her mouth, another woman with tears in her eyes came up to me on my right, expressing the same appreciation because her dad died on January 13, 1996! All three of us stood there in awe at the situation and praised Jesus! Was it a coincidence that we all lost a parent on January 13? I think not. In fact, I know not!

God is in control. He knows everything before and hereafter. He is God of All. This was truly evident that night. I praise Christ Jesus and thank Him for his unending love, mercy, grace, and peace that surpass all understanding! Amen!

Do not be anxious about anything, but in everything, by prayer and petition, with thanksgiving, present your requests to God. And the peace of God, which transcends all understanding, will guard your hearts and your minds in Christ Jesus (Philippians 4:6–7).

BLESS ME INDEED

The day finally arrived in my life when I was going to face major surgery. It took me away from my position at work for over six- to eight weeks. After informing my manager of my medical leave, I began preparing for one of my associates to fulfill my duties during my absence. I'd been talking to men all across the United States who were in their final stages of cancer. Every week, I would call each of these men to assess their pain level while taking a new medication. Talking with someone week after week, you tend to develop a personal relationship.

This particular week, my calls were not only to assess their pain level but also to let them know I'd be on medical leave over the next six to eight weeks. I told them that someone new would be calling them weekly. I wanted them to know in advance so they wouldn't feel uncomfortable during my absence. While I spoke to one man named Mr. Montgomery, informing him of my upcoming absence, he said, "Ellen, would it be all right for me to pray for you before we hang up?"

I said, "Absolutely." My heart was pierced to the depths of my being to think this man who was dying wanted to pray for me.

After his prayer, I thanked him and told him to take real good care of himself and that I'd be talking with him in a few weeks. I returned to work approximately eight weeks later. I began making my calls. I called Mr. Montgomery, and his wife answered. I asked if I could speak to her husband, but she informed me that he had passed away just a few weeks before my call. I was devastated! I was almost speechless. I told Mrs. Montgomery how sorry I was to hear about her husband and how much I enjoyed talking with him. She thanked me and told me how much he looked forward to my call each week. As I hung up the phone, the tears fell uncontrollably down my cheeks. I felt a hand on my shoulder, and it was a lady who sat on the other side of my cubicle who heard my conversation. She came over to comfort me.

I couldn't stop thinking about Mr. Montgomery throughout the remainder of the day. My heart was so heavy I wrote down his number in my phonebook, and when I arrived home that evening, I called his wife. I reminded her of who I was, and I told her I felt led to call and tell her how much her husband meant to me—how he prayed for me and how he touched my life. She was so appreciative. We talked many times from that point on. We had so much in common, mainly Jesus Christ. We could just talk and talk about the Lord and His truth. As we continued to speak over the months ahead, we continued to learn more about each other. One thing that really spoke to my heart was that her name was Louise. This was also my mom's name. Her birthday was October 4, and my mom's birthday was November 4.

I grew closer to Mrs. Montgomery. It helped to fill the void of losing my mother several years before. I ended up sending her a written copy of my testimony, along with a few other articles, revealing the works of the Lord in my life. She called me to say how much they blessed her heart and wanted my permission to share them with her congregation. What a blessing that was to me! I also remember one day in particular when I went to the Christian bookstore to pick up a few cards I needed. While I was in the checkout line, I noticed the books displayed on the best-seller rack next to me. I picked up this tiny book titled *The Prayer of Jabez* by Bruce Wilkinson.

As I read the intro, I wanted to buy the book, but I heard this small voice in my spirit say, "You don't need to be buying any books right now," so I put it back on the shelf. I paid for my cards and headed home.

As I drove into my driveway, I stopped to get my mail out of my mailbox as I do every day. I received a small package from Mrs. Montgomery. I could hardly wait to get inside and open it to see what she had sent me. My eyes just about popped out of my head; it was *The Prayer of Jabez*. She wrote on the front cover:

Dear Ellen,

May God bless you INDEED!

With love,
Mrs. Louise Montgomery

Was this a coincidence? Absolutely not! I immediately called her to tell her what just happened and how the Lord really used her to make sure I could read that little book.

After reading that book, the Holy Spirit led me to purchase many copies and anonymously distribute them to each family within my church at the time. Let's just say *The Prayer of Jabez* was the talk of our church for quite some time. What a wonderful little book.

> Jabez cried out to the God of Israel, "Oh, that you would bless me and enlarge my territory! Let your hand be with me, and keep me from harm so that I will be free from pain." And God granted his request (1 Chronicles 4:10).

KEEPING YOUR EYES ON JESUS

I started attending this little church I was led to seven years before. I started going to the 11:00 a.m. service. After attending this service for a couple of months, I was led to go to Sunday school. I hadn't been in Sunday school since I was a little girl. To my surprise, I really enjoyed it. I felt such a sweet spirit in this church. I also started attending Wednesday-night services. I found myself anticipating going to church. This was the first time in over seven years I felt Jesus planting me where He wanted me to grow.

I started to think about joining this congregation. I prayed about it and pleaded with the Lord to direct me in the way He wanted me to go. The church was preparing for revival services starting with a week of cottage prayer meetings. I was asked to sing during the revival. Because I hadn't sung since being diagnosed with asthma, I allowed the devil to weigh me down with fear. I attended the cottage prayer meetings and found myself enjoying the fellowship with other believers. I continued to thank the Lord for this and seek God's perfect will about joining this congregation.

One night, after a prayer meeting, I stopped by a nearby grocery store to pick up a few things. While in the store, I spoke to this lady who was looking for an express lane. The man told her there wasn't one open, and she said, "Oh, I was just trying to find my way around. I just moved here." She thanked the man and came and stood behind me. I noticed she only had a box of Band-Aids, so I told her she could go ahead of me. She said, "Are you sure?"

I said, "Certainly. No problem."

She said, "I've been moving all day, and my hands are all torn to bits."

And sure enough, they were. I asked her where she was moving to, and she said they were actually building a house in Wakefield, which is a very exclusive housing development. I told her how beautiful I thought it was there. I asked her where she moved from, and she said Charlotte. I then asked her if she found a church here yet. She said she hadn't, so I invited her to the church I was attending. She asked me the name of the church, so I wrote it down with the directions for her. Her name was June, and she said she would see me there. I said, "I sure hope so."

She said, "You will!"

I felt so wonderful and just praised the Lord on my way home for allowing me to invite someone to church.

The next evening, at a cottage prayer meeting, the pastor read some scripture out of the Bible, and we were discussing it. Just before we went into our prayer session, he ended the discussion with these words (I will never forget them because I felt as if the Lord had put his arms around me at that very moment he spoke them): "We are all called to be witnesses for the Lord. We never know when we could be witnessing, say, to someone who has just moved here from Charlotte."

When he said Charlotte, I melted! I wanted to speak up and say, "Hey, Pastor, were you at the Food Lion last night or what?" Isn't the Lord amazing?

Sunday was the homecoming for the church, and it was also the day they planned to kick off the revival services. I figured, *What better day to join than on homecoming.* After all, I felt as if I was coming home, especially since I hadn't been an actual member of a church since I was about eighteen years old. I became a member of this little church on August 8, 1999.

Now came the Monday night that I was to sing three songs back to back. My palms were sweating, and I was nervous. I had a dream the night before as follows:

> I got to the church and handed my tapes to the sound technician when I realized I brought the wrong tapes! I picked them up by mistake. In fact, I didn't even know the songs, and there wasn't enough time to go back home and get the right ones. I went up to the pulpit area and picked up the microphone. It had a short cord, so I had to bend over to sing.

When I woke up that Monday morning, I was very distraught! The night came so quickly. It was time to sing. I arrived at the church and gave the sound technician my tapes and shared my dream with some of the women in the sanctuary. We all laughed and said, "It's gonna be all right."

As I stood waiting for the music to start, it couldn't be heard. I found myself bending down over the speaker to hear a familiar note to begin singing, but the cord on the microphone wouldn't reach! It was then this small voice (the Holy Spirit) said, "Start singing. You are singing to me, not to them. The music doesn't matter." It took me a moment to get my sole concentration on the Lord, but when I did, I felt strength beyond my comprehension. The music was never right, but then again, maybe it was. The music actually stopped on the last song as I kept singing. I was determined Satan wouldn't win.

As I sat down, the minister holding the revival meetings took his place at the pulpit. When he began preaching, I remember him saying how we needed to be a witness for Christ Jesus whether it be down the road at the Food Lion or wherever. Again, that was confirmation to me! Once again, I felt the Lord's arms around me.

The next morning, when I woke up and got ready for work, I

realized a few things that still make me want to shout, praise the Lord, and continually smile:

1. Even if I didn't bring the wrong music, I didn't need music.
2. The microphone cord wasn't too short when standing straight up for the Lord. It only became too short when I bent over and took my eyes off him.
3. The words to any song are the most important, not the beat or the loudness of the music. It's the content, which is the message.[1]

Seven years prior to that Monday night, the same thing happened to me while singing for about two hundred people in a church (Bible application class). I cried and actually felt anger toward the sound technician. I also felt embarrassed and humiliated. The congregation tried to encourage me by telling me how my singing had touched them. It was hard to hear them because I couldn't get past feelings of hurt. I don't know about you, but for me, it's really hard to see when my eyes are on me.

On Monday night, seven years later as I mentioned earlier, I felt the Lord was in control, and the power in Him gave me strength and joy that can't be explained. All I know even now is that I love the Lord with all my heart, and depending on Him is all I can really be sure of in my life. I guess you could say that I actually started dying to myself that day. Praise the Lord!

> May I never boast except in the cross of our Lord Jesus Christ, through which the world has been crucified to me, and I to the world (Galatians 6:14).

---

[1] Some beats and rhythms are demonically inspired and will bring a curse on those who listen to them. This is not the essence of what the author has mentioned here. However, it is an important footnote in case there might be any confusion with some who may feel that the author's statement gives license to listen to any type of beat or rhythm. Be aware!

STAND UP, STAND UP FOR JESUS

I was invited one Saturday night during the Christmas holidays to come sing and fellowship with a group of people from a very prominent church in the area. As the night came to a close and their pastor left, a lady whose home we were visiting started showing us her collection of Disney characters. As she pointed out her very large display, she mentioned she wouldn't show them while the pastor was there because he preaches a lot on the subject of supporting Walt Disney World in relation to homosexuality. The woman and her husband I came with said, "Oh, there's nothing wrong with collecting them. It's not like you're worshipping them or anything."

I stood there, and all I could say was that I read about Walt Disney World being a supporter of the homosexual agenda from the American Family Association website. [1]

No sooner had I said that than another lady said, "Well, I can't really comment because my husband is in seminary."

I thought to myself, *Husband in seminary? What does that have to do with anything? Do you not have a mind of your own?*

I was really conflicted. I felt I should've defended their pastor, not to mention Christ Jesus. That's the problem now; people don't see anything wrong with supporting something as long as it's what *they want*. In reality, we're called to sacrifice. Deep in my spirit, I believe this means to give up something we really want to bring praise and glory to our Lord and Savior Jesus Christ.

We live in a society where compromise and tolerance have become the number one principles in life. Whatever happened to putting Jesus Christ and his teachings first? It's like Duke Chapel at Duke University located in North Carolina changing *marriage* to *union* to make same-sex marriages acceptable. This can fool only liberal people who, in their ongoing efforts to be "tolerant" and "open-minded," are tolerant and open-minded to Satan.

When we sacrifice the *truth* of Jesus Christ to have the things we want in this life just because it's easier to go with the flow rather than to take a stand for Jesus, then we deserve the punishment that awaits us. We're called to be witnesses and disciples of men, not pacifists and enablers of Satan. No one said it was easy to be a follower of Jesus. We should already know this because of what our Lord and Savior faced after He entered this world.

At the time of this story, we were approaching Christmas, the day we celebrate the birth of Jesus, the one who sacrificed everything for each of us so we could have eternal life. Isn't it about time we start standing up for Jesus? He did His part; now it's our turn to do our part. Jesus is the reason for the Christmas season. Jesus is the reason we have hope. He who stands for nothing will fall for anything, and he who stands for anything will simply fall. As the old gospel hymn "Stand Up, Stand Up for Jesus" by George Duffield Jr. goes:

Stand up, stand up for Jesus,
Ye soldiers of the cross,
Lift high His royal banner,
It must not suffer loss,
From victory unto victory, His army shall He lead,
Till every foe is vanquished and Christ is Lord in
   deed.
Stand up, stand up for Jesus,
The trumpet call obey,
Forth to the mighty conflict,
In this His glorious day,

Ye who are men now serve Him against
    unnumbered foes,
Let courage rise with danger and strength to
    strength oppose.
Stand up, stand up for Jesus, stand in His strength
    alone,
The arm of flesh will fail you,
Ye dare not trust your own,
Put on the gospel armor,
Each piece put on with prayer, where duty calls or
    danger,
Be never wanting there
Stand up, stand up for Jesus,
The strife will not be long,
This day the noise of battle,
The next the victor's song,
To him who overcometh,
A crown of life shall be,
He with the king of glory shall reign eternally.

IT'S TIME TO TAKE A STAND!

Awake thou that sleepest, and arise from the dead.
—Ephesians 5:14b

People are talking everywhere—talking about the way the world is going and the way many people who claim to be Christians are going. For example, the stance that some of our more traditional churches are taking on subjects such as same-sex unions, abortion, tolerance, and acceptance. Many of these denominations have split or are in the process of splitting apart because of these issues. People are asking, "What is happening?" I would like to say it's time to take a stand and speak up for what we know is right before it's too late! God has not called us to be complacent at a time like this!

I attended an interdenominational women's prayer conference held at one of the mainstream churches in the area. The theme for the conference was "Be Still and Know." I was really looking forward to this prayer conference since I attended one just last year and found it to be very inspirational and mission-oriented.

The conference lasted from Friday night until Saturday afternoon. A friend and I were the only two people from our church to attend. When we arrived, we found we didn't know anyone there. Just before the program began, I saw a friend of mine I hadn't seen for quite some time. We briefly talked and set a date for me to go visit her and her family. This was a pleasant surprise.

The conference began with the singing of a few songs. The songs chosen were somber—songs I didn't assume were fitting for a prayerful evening. In between a few of the songs, a woman from the organization stood up at the podium to tell us about the women who were speaking that night.

The first woman she spoke of was a pastor from another state who traveled to the conference with a friend of hers and that she would be coming shortly to do the scripture reading and prayer. The other woman was a registered nurse (RN) and chaplain from one of the major hospitals in the area who was the keynote speaker.

The pastor took her place in front of the podium and introduced her housemate to everyone. Then she began to tell how blessed she was to have this person as her housemate and how wonderful it was to have someone to look forward to coming home in the evening— that is, someone who could fix meals and sew that occasional button on when needed. By this time, I was beginning to feel a little uncomfortable—if you know what I mean (especially with what's going on within the mainstream denominations in reference to the acceptance of homosexuality). She read the scripture and said a prayer, and then she took her seat out in the congregation next to her housemate.

Next, the RN took her place behind the podium. She spoke on a book titled *Women's Wisdom and Women's Bodies*. I failed to see how this secular book played a part in the "Be Still and Know" theme, although there were some points she brought out in dealing with the lives of individuals that were valid. I became really puzzled right after the valid points when the speaker began talking about our solar plexus, second brain, and how it evolved into one brain! Are you lost yet? I was!

By this time, I was really wondering, *What on earth is going on?* I couldn't help but wonder if we were getting ready to go into the theory of evolution or not. The conference ended, and my friend and I gathered up our belongings to leave.

When we got into my vehicle, the first thing we did was discuss the night's activities. I was relieved to hear my friend thought the same things I did about the pastor and the main speaker. It was just as disturbing to her as it was to me. We were in agreement that we didn't desire to go back on Saturday morning.

My old friend I'd seen at the conference called me at the end of the following week to reschedule our get-together because of a conflict. I asked her how she enjoyed the conference, and she was just as bewildered as my other friend and I were. She had the same thoughts as we did. I felt that if the three of us received the same impression, then we probably weren't the only ones.

I couldn't get this off my mind! I talked to a minister friend of mine, and he suggested I contact Mrs. Wilson (not her real name), who was the lady on the committee that planned the conference. He gave me her phone number and told me she would be expecting my call.

I prayed and asked the Lord to direct my words. Then I placed the call and introduced myself. I told Mrs. Wilson I didn't know any other way to tell her what I felt, except to just come right out and say it, so that's exactly what I did! She became very defensive, saying she couldn't imagine why anyone would, or could, have come to such a conclusion! She informed me she knew the pastor for several years and that what I was saying was simply not the case! She continued by telling me what a hard life this pastor had in the past, how she even went through some chemotherapy, and how everyone within the church organization for this conference was so happy to see she had someone to live with and help her. She said, in fact, that the woman the pastor lived with was a widow and a wonderful lady.

Mrs. Wilson then told me sometimes people look too hard for things that aren't there by being just a little too suspicious. I assured her nothing of the kind had ever entered my mind until that night. I also told her that the churches that were now in the middle of the big splits over the homosexual agenda probably wish they questioned things more if they had it to do all over again. I told her I hoped that the homosexual agenda didn't rear its ugly head and infiltrate her church.

She asked me, "What do you think we're supposed to do? Kick those people out?"

I told her, "You've just said it yourself, calling them 'those people,' which tells me you don't consider them to be the same as yourself." I told her she was absolutely correct in her thinking because they weren't like her. I said, "You repent of your sins, hopefully, but homosexuals (who continue practicing homosexual acts) don't. They don't feel they're doing anything wrong and . . . that's the difference!"

She said, "Well, I hope they don't infiltrate your church either."

I assured her if they did, it wouldn't be because I was afraid to question something for fear of appearing too suspicious. I thanked her for her time and told her to have a good night. It's my prayer Mrs. Wilson will share this concern with the pastor, as she may want to preface her introduction regarding her housemate in such a way as to remove any appearance of evil in the future, assuming I misunderstood, of course.

Looking back, I can't help but wonder if I should've taken my concern directly to the speaker herself. At the time, being new to the Word of God, I just wanted to go through the appropriate channels recommended by my minister friend whom I highly respected. In the future, however, my approach will be different, and I will go directly to the person with my concern as Matthew 18:15–17 instructs.

After I spoke with Mrs. Wilson, I then called Mrs. Jones (not her real name) from my church, who's a part of this same organization, to let her know what I had said in case she was ever approached about this situation. She felt if Mrs. Wilson knew this woman for several years, then she was sure she knew the truth about her and that this woman was not a homosexual (i.e., lesbian). I told her she was probably right, but I just wanted people to be aware that things aren't always as they seem. I told Mrs. Jones that homosexuals can be your friend for years, and you'd never suspect they were living the "homosexual lifestyle." I told her this is how they gain acceptance. (I've been there, I know).

It's so much easier to become friends with someone and gain their love and trust before knowing about their lifestyle. After all, one's sex life is not something most Christians go around discussing in public. As a usual thing, you never give that part of someone's life a second thought because it's sacred. In fact, that's just something not discussed. Period. This is the door that leads a person into the liberal stand of tolerance. It's with this liberal stand Satan inserts his foot of deceit and starts the ball rolling on "same-sex unions," which are being embraced by some evangelicals and splitting congregations in many areas of our world today.

Although I never found out for sure if this pastor was a lesbian, the fact remains we need to wake up and realize we're all susceptible to coming in contact with the devil and his schemes. We don't have to be lured into his web of deceit. We do have a choice, and we don't have to ignore what's going on if we really want and expect to win this battle (1 Timothy 2:12–14)!

We need to quit hiding and get our heads out of the sand! It's time to wake up and take a stand for what we know to be right and true rather than sweeping it under the carpet as many of us have been doing! We need to get rid of the mentality that things like this can never happen in our churches—or in our own homes for that matter. It's time to take a stand and be counted, ready for combat.

> Finally, be strong in the Lord and in His mighty power. Put on the full armor of God so that you can take your stand against the devil's schemes. For our struggle is not against flesh and blood, but against the rulers, against the authorities, against the powers of this dark world and against the spiritual forces of evil in the heavenly realms. Therefore, put on the full armor of God, so that when the day of evil comes, you may be able to stand your ground,

and after you have done everything, to stand. Stand firm then, with the belt of truth buckled around your waist, with the breastplate of righteousness in place, and with your feet fitted with the readiness that comes from the gospel of peace. In addition to all this, take up the shield of faith, with which you can extinguish all the flaming arrows of the evil one. Take the helmet of salvation and the sword of the Spirit, which is the Word of God. And pray in the Spirit on all occasions with all kinds of prayers and requests. With this in mind, be alert and always keep on praying for all the saints (Ephesians 6:10–18).

ALL THINGS WORK TOGETHER!

After eight years, our pastor decided to leave. This was his first church, and now he felt led in another direction. He wasn't leaving for another church or leaving the community. He didn't have to leave for theft, indecent acts, or anything like that. He was just changing his field of ministry, which he couldn't discuss at that time because of a couple of things in the works.

This was very understandable to me but not to everyone. I was approached by a couple of people in the church who were really upset, even to the point of crying and feeling a little angry. I shared my thoughts with them as well as with the pastor.

They were the following:

1. I was sad until I thought about the Lord orchestrating the pastor's move. Then I got excited for him, his family, and their future.
2. I shed tears because my human side was going to miss him in the pulpit. Then my tears turned to joy and excitement waiting to see who the Lord would bless our church with next! In fact, I started thanking Him at that very moment for who He was sending to our church.
3. I knew we had some new people in our church who were thinking about joining our congregation. I also knew they

were watching us to see how we would respond to our pastor leaving.

This, to me, is a perfect example of 1 Thessalonians 5:16–18, which says, "Be joyful always, pray continually; give thanks in all circumstances, for this is God's will for you in Christ Jesus."

I thanked the Lord for this attitude, especially when one Sunday after church I overheard someone approach this lady whom I shared these thoughts with just a day or two ago. The woman walked up to her crying and said, "This is such a sad, sad day!"

I couldn't help but rejoice in the Lord when I heard her respond by saying, "Well, not really when you realize God is in control. In fact, it's kind of exciting!"

Isn't God good? It's wonderful to see how He uses each of His children to be an encouragement and to learn from one another no matter the circumstance. I just praise and thank Him for being the center of my very being, and I rest in knowing that nothing can separate us from the love of God that is in Christ Jesus our Lord. Amen!

And we know that all things work together for good
to them that love God, to them who are the called
according to his purpose (Romans 8:28).

GOD WILL GIVE US THE DESIRES OF OUR HEARTS

I really don't exactly know how to begin this story except by saying I'm sure everyone has relatives that, for one reason or another, you haven't known very well. Some relatives you probably never knew. Such is the situation in this story for me.

Growing up in the country with my aunts and uncles living down the road and across the field was a wonderful time in my life. Having these relatives around me helped me to get through the years of my youth. They furnished the love I needed to survive in a home where love was not displayed.

All my relatives have passed away except for a very few. One was my aunt Elsie, whom I never knew very well. Growing up, I was never allowed to go over to her house very much because my mom always had chores or something for me to do. She felt I didn't have any business going over there. As a little girl, I would sometimes sneak over there for a few minutes but not very often.

Both of my parents went on to be with the Lord, and I found myself without any family. What family I had had become estranged just before my mom died. I've prayed about my estranged family in the hope that one day we would reunite.

I sold the homeplace (my childhood home), which was very difficult for me since it was where I was born and raised. I came to the decision to sell it after much prayer because I couldn't keep up my current home and maintain my homeplace some seventy miles away. However, I kept the farmland, which I rented out for crops to be grown.

Since selling the house, I had surgery, which left me incapacitated for a while. It could've been a very depressing time in my life, but thanks to the Lord, He provided me with a lot of visits and cards from people. One card, in particular, was from my aunt Elsie. It was such a sweet card, and the little girl on the front of it reminded me of myself. I was so touched. She heard from a neighbor in the community back home about my surgery and wanted me to know she was thinking of me.

After healing from my surgery, which was the first of October, I headed back to the homeplace to transplant some rose bushes that my mom dearly loved. I went to bring them to my house and set them out in my yard. When I arrived, I stopped to visit one of the ladies in the community whom I refer to as Aunt Helen (actually she is not related to me except in the Lord). She told me I should wait until it got a little colder and they became dormant, so they wouldn't die. I agreed to do what she told me because she raised rose bushes. In fact, she was the one who gave my mom the ones I came to transplant to my current home.

After visiting her for a while, I left and proceeded to my homeplace so I could tell the guy who bought the house that I wouldn't be getting the rose bushes that day. I took a detour around the block and drove by the house of one of my estranged family members. Their front door was open. There was a part of me that wanted to stop. The Holy Spirit said, "No, don't stop. Now is not the time." As I drove on down the road, I told the Lord I was sad because I wanted to have contact with relatives that I could talk to and be close with—someone who knew my parents, someone I could laugh and cry with.

Driving down the road, I passed the house of my aunt Elsie, whom I never really got to know. I saw my cousin outside cooking what looked to be a pig on the cooker. There were a few cars in the yard, and I wondered what was going on. I figured it was such a pretty day they must be having a cookout. I continued on down the road and pulled into the yard of my homeplace to visit with Doug, the guy who bought the house. I told him about delaying the rose bush transplant for a few more months, and he was fine with that decision. I left his house and went to visit the lady who rented my farm before heading back to my home. As we sat talking, I mentioned I saw my cousin out in the yard cooking a pig. She said that it was my aunt's eightieth birthday, and all the family was there to celebrate. When she said eightieth birthday, the card my aunt sent me flashed before my eyes.

All of a sudden, I felt like I should go over there and wish her a happy birthday. After all, she thought enough of me to send me a card. It was so long since I'd seen my cousins I knew I wouldn't recognize them. When I pulled into the yard, there were so many more vehicles than when I first arrived. I wanted to turn around and leave. I didn't because it was too late. I was already there.

I parked my truck and went into the house. People were everywhere. I didn't know a soul. Finally, I saw my aunt Elsie out on the back deck with her walking stick in one hand and her daughter with her other hand, helping her to walk. My aunt seemed so happy to see me. She said I really made her birthday. She made me feel so special on what was *her* special day. Then another lady came out the door and said my name. I had no idea who she was. She told me she was my cousin. She was the oldest of Aunt Elsie's children. I saw cousins I hadn't seen in many years. Most of them, I'd never recognized on the street. It was really good to reconnect with everyone.

By this time, I felt I should leave since they were getting ready to eat, and I didn't come to eat. I tried to get out of the door to leave, but someone was standing in front of the door, and I couldn't get out. I tried to go another way, but people were crowding in on me to join hands for a prayer before eating. I was stuck. There was nothing left for me to do but hold the person's hand on each side of me and bow my head.

As I stood there listening to this young man pray such a sweet prayer, I thought how wonderful it was to know that this family knew the Lord. This was something I never really knew about them. After the prayer, I thought, *Now I can leave.* Wrong again. One of my cousins walked up and introduced me to her husband, who was the man next to me blocking the door. Then another cousin handed me a plate. The next thing I knew, we were all sitting, eating, and talking. It was wonderful!

We talked about my parents. One cousin told me about the time I was born and how she used to look at me in the bassinet and how she always knew that I was a special child. We finished eating, gathered around the piano, and started singing my aunt Elsie's favorite hymns. It was wonderful!

As I was leaving, my cousins hugged me tight and then looked me dead in the eyes and said, "We are your family, Ellen, and we love you unconditionally." I felt the Lord put his arms around me at that very moment. We exchanged phone numbers and email addresses, and I left to go home.

I arrived there that day at approximately 2:45 p.m. and didn't leave until about 7:00 p.m. I was so full of joy when I left that the trip home didn't seem long at all. After reflecting on the day, I realized the Lord answered my prayer. He allowed me to have a family who also belonged to Him. I thank and praise Him to this day for continuing to give me the desires of my heart. It's awesome to me how I made the trip that day to transplant a couple of rose bushes when, in reality, the only thing transplanted was me.

Since that day, my aunt Elsie has gone on to be with the Lord. My cousins sold their homeplace and moved away. I may never see them again on this side of heaven, but I'm so thankful Jesus allowed me to have that one day with them. My once-estranged family has now been reunited. I will forever praise Jesus for granting the desire of my heart!

Delight yourself in the Lord and he will give you the desires of your heart (Psalm 37:4).

And I will do whatever you ask in my name so that the Son can bring glory to the Father, You can ask for anything in my name and I will do it (John 14:13–14).

Praise the Lord!

DO NOT FEAR

I'd like to share with you the obstacle of fear and how it attempts to weigh you down when following through on what the Lord is leading you to do. How many times have I been led to step out in faith and take on a project I wasn't sure I could do or even if it was really the Lord leading me to do it? Not to mention, the possibility of failing! Sound familiar? Have you ever been plagued with thoughts like these? Thoughts like, suppose I fail and don't succeed? Everyone will be looking at me. They will say things like "I can't believe she thought she could do that to begin with. She didn't have any business taking that position. Look what a mess she made."

Ever had these feelings? Rest assured, when those thoughts come into your mind, they are not of the Lord. Fear is not of the Lord. Period! "The Spirit you received does not make you slaves, so that you live in fear again; rather, the Spirit you received brought about your adoption to sonship. And by him we cry, Abba, Father" (Romans 8:15).

I'd like to share with you the recording process of my CD. But first, I want to make a few statements and ask that you follow me closely. I've known for many years now that one day I would be sharing my testimony of conversion in a massive way. In fact, when my life changed, the Lord revealed to me in my spirit this would occur. I never knew how, when, or where but only that it would happen.

Now, getting back to the recording process of my CD. The Lord gave me eleven original songs, and He led me to record them. He provided the name for my CD and ministry. My CD is titled *Jesus, Heart of the Matter*. My ministry name is Heart of Jesus Ministries. He led me to a Christian recording studio in Fort Worth, Texas. I couldn't help but think this sure is a long way to go to record a CD. Nevertheless, I obeyed and started to work on the arrangements. Many people were asking me left and right, "Why are you going way out there to record your CD?" All I could tell them was I felt the Lord leading me in that direction.

I know people were looking at me and wondering if I'd lost my mind, but I knew deep down in my spirit I had to go. I got everything in order. I made hotel and plane reservations as Satan attempted to discourage me from going. For example, the manager of a Christian bookstore told me when I finished my CD they would stock it for sale. I stopped by to tell them I'd be bringing them my packaged CD in a few weeks. However, they told me things had changed and they could no longer stock any CDs from local artists because they weren't on their distribution list.

When I reminded them what they had told me, they just apologized and sent me on my way. I was crushed. In fact, Satan took full advantage of the situation; but then again, I allowed him. The things going through my mind were discouraging. Things like no need to spend all that money making that CD because nobody is going to buy it.

Tears began to flow down my face. I called on the Lord, and immediately, I remembered there was another Christian bookstore that told me they would also stock my CD. So I headed down the road to see them. As I walked into the store, I checked out the racks to make sure they still had CDs by local artists displayed. I was relieved to find they did. I felt confident at that moment. I asked to speak to the manager. She came toward me, and I met her halfway down the aisle. I reminded her who I was and told her about my CD. She immediately stopped and informed me of the same thing that the manager of the first Christian bookstore had told me.

By this time, it was all I could do to hold it together. I barely managed to get out the door before the tears started falling uncontrollably. As I walked to my truck, all I could hear in my spirit was "See, nobody is going to sell your CD. You might as well not bother going to Fort Worth. Save your money and forget about recording this CD!" I was so distraught. As I sat in my truck, I called a friend on my cell phone for encouragement. She told me that Satan was a liar and that the Lord didn't bring me this far to just leave me here. I thanked the Lord and praised Him for a friend like her! I composed myself.

As I headed down the road, I remembered there was one more Christian bookstore that said they would stock my CD. I started to go to that store but decided I would just go home instead. I was discouraged enough for one day. While I was driving down the road, the words came to me, "It's not about me."

By the time I arrived home, I finished writing my twelfth song. I called the studio in Fort Worth and asked the producer if we could add another song to the CD. He told me to get it in the mail to him pronto. So I did. This song really helped me to get on that plane. I realized that none of this was about me. It was all about Jesus!!

It was the Friday morning before the day I was supposed to leave for Fort Worth. As I turned into the parking lot at work, I saw this huge jet taking off from our local airport. Immediately, I started to sing the words, "I'm flying high." By the time I reached my desk, I wrote the first verse of song number thirteen. The songs just kept coming. At that moment, I felt more assured I was meant to record the CD.

Now the day came, and I was boarding the plane headed to Fort Worth, Texas. About an hour into the trip and thousands of feet in the air, fear came all over me. I started praying, "Lord, am I really doing what you want me to do? I want it to be your perfect will!" At that moment, I was interrupted by the flight attendant as she said, "Pretzels?" I accepted the bag along with a beverage. I continued talking to the Lord as I ate the pretzels, pleading with Him to let me know I was doing what He wanted me to do. I finished my prayer and my pretzels and balled up the bag.

All of a sudden, the remainder of the song "I'm Flying High" filled my mind. I grabbed my pad and pen and finished the song before we landed in Fort Worth.

As I sat waiting to land, I heard this still, small voice say, "Look at that pretzel bag." I straightened the bag out, and when I realized what it said, I started to cry tears of joy. The word *heartzels* was written on the bag. I found out a little later in the trip that this snack was making its debut in Texas. Frito-Lay joined the American Heart Association to launch this new snack. Coincidence? I think not! I had the bag laminated for safekeeping. I never want to forget that trip and how the Lord spoke to me that day. Talk about continuous prayer; it was me and the Lord all the way during that plane ride.

When we landed in Fort Worth, fear crept back in. It was a big airport, and I needed to find the shuttle so I could pick up my rental car as well as find my way to the hotel. I started talking to the Lord again. Calmness came over me. I found the shuttle. I found my car and headed for the hotel. After I checked into the hotel and got settled, I called the producer, and he gave me directions to the studio. I was so excited! I grabbed a bite to eat and spent some more time with the Lord in prayer. I slept like a baby that night.

The next morning, I arrived at the studio where the producer met me in the parking lot. He came out, opened my car door, and introduced himself. We entered the studio, and there before me was a room full of musicians. After all the introductions were made, the producer said, "Let's begin with a word of prayer!" At that moment, I knew I was in the right place. I praised my Lord with Thanksgiving in my heart all day long!

We were in the studio day and night from Monday morning until Thursday afternoon when the producer took me out to eat for the first time since arriving. We talked and shared things about our lives and growing up. All of a sudden, I was led to share my testimony with him. I must have had a strange look on my face because he asked if I was all right. I told him I didn't know why but I felt led to share my testimony with him. This was really odd because my testimony was the furthest thing from my mind. He told me to go ahead; he would like to hear it. When I finished, he told me my testimony was really powerful and that he knew someone who would really like to talk to me if I'd be willing. I agreed.

The next thing I knew, I was being interviewed by the producer of a Christian television program in Fort Worth. The Lord knew all along the reasons for me going to Forth Worth. If I hadn't been obedient, if I'd given in to Satan's fear tactics and not continued seeking Jesus and stepping out in faith, I would've missed this opportunity as well as creating a wonderful original CD glorifying Jesus! What a glorious experience!

As you're reading this now, you may be experiencing the Lord leading you to do something out of your comfort zone. Pray. Seek Him and His guidance. Don't allow fear to latch on to you. Shake it loose! Remember, fear is not of the Lord. Above all else, remember, "It's not about me." It's about Jesus Christ and how people see Him in you and what you do for the glory of God and His kingdom!

When I returned home from Fort Worth, I stopped by the Christian bookstore, and they were only too happy to stock my CD for sale. They still stock it today with other items available from Heart of Jesus Ministries. Praise the Lord! I know He's not finished with me yet!

> Being confident of this, that he who began a good work in you will carry it on to completion until the day of Christ Jesus (Philippians 1:6).

AMAZING MERCY
AND GRACE

It was a warm day in April when I received an invitation to attend a music workshop in Nashville, Tennessee. I didn't think I could afford to make the trip as it was over a thousand miles round-trip, but regardless, I felt I was supposed to go. So long story short, I packed my car and took off through the mountains of North Carolina and Tennessee, just me and the Lord. Boy, were those mountains beautiful.

I previously lived in Nashville, Tennessee, for a few years. I was excited to return after being gone for close to twenty years. When I arrived, I got settled in my hotel room and then set out to find Belmont College. I thought I remembered it being close to where I used to live, and sure enough, it was right where I remembered it. I drove down Sixteenth Avenue (Music Row) and stopped at the Brown Stone where I used to live.

As I stood in the courtyard, I could see Belmont College at the end of the street. I realized I was standing in the very same place where I once lived and served the devil by drinking, taking drugs, and living a life of promiscuity; and here I was, serving my Lord! This was a time of special communion between my Savior and me. I was in great awe of how I'd come full circle. God is amazing and full of mercy!

I attended seminars from eight the next morning until six in the evening. The day was wonderful. There were about fifty people like me who were eager to soak up all the information provided for us. Many people in the Christian music industry were there to share their experiences, as well as tools to further our service to the Lord through music. It was a wonderful experience, and I'm so glad that I followed through by making the trip.

There were a few people who couldn't believe I was going to take the trip alone. If I'd given in to the fear they were projecting, I would've stayed at home and missed several blessings. I especially enjoyed driving back through the mountains. It was downhill all the way, and it was so much fun driving my little car (2006 Scion xB). I didn't have to hit my brakes—not even once! It was like being on a ride at an amusement park.

Upon returning home, I started to put the tools I learned into motion. I started surfing the net to find independent radio stations. I would listen to each station to determine if they were playing my style of music or not. This way, I would know whether to contact them about airing my CD. I was listening to one station while searching for others when, lo and behold, this song started to play on this radio station out of Washington State. It was this woman I was searching for since my mom went to be with the Lord back in 1998! Someone gave me a copy of her music, and it was such a blessing to me during my mom's last days. Her music inspired me in such a way I felt the presence of my Lord envelop me. I only had her first name and couldn't make out her last name on the cassette because my copy was so badly worn. I was elated!

I almost gave up hope that I'd ever be able to get a fresh, clean copy of her work. The radio station provided her name and website. Now I have a wonderful brand-new CD that continues to be an inspiration in my life to this day. Check her out at www.loriwilke.com. The title of the CD is *Here I Am*.

I'm so thankful the Lord allowed me to go back to Nashville because it helped me realize where I was and where I am now, which was only made possible by His marvelous mercy and grace. Also, through this experience, He allowed me to find Lori Wilke, whose music stirred my heart to the depth of my soul at a time when I was so weak and needed the strength of my Lord. Praise God from whom *all* blessings flow!

> All of us also lived among them at one time, gratifying the cravings of our sinful nature and following its desires and thoughts. Like the rest, we were by nature objects of wrath. But because of His great love for us, God, who is rich in mercy, made us alive with Christ even when we were dead in transgressions—it is by grace you have been saved (Ephesians 2:3–5).

MY PEACE I GIVE UNTO YOU

It was early one summer while living in a relationship with a woman when I experienced the Lord Jesus Christ drawing me to Himself but didn't realize it was happening. I just started living with my fourth partner. After she moved in, she decided to go see her dad who lived in Canada, where she was born. Before she left, she gave me a cassette of instrumental music. It played it over and over several times before it stopped. After she left, I listened to this instrumental music every night before going to bed. In fact, this music would lull me to sleep. I had no idea what the name of this music was or where it came from. All I knew is I felt peaceful and content when listening to it every night at bedtime. I couldn't hear it enough.

My partner returned after spending several weeks with her dad, and the cassette disappeared, never to be heard or seen again. This woman lived with me for approximately five years until one day she informed me that she was moving out. One year prior to her moving, I called out to the Lord for the first time in my life since the age of eighteen. I asked if He was really there to get me out of this lifestyle because I wasn't content and didn't know how to put an end to the life I chose.

Needless to say, when my partner informed me she was leaving, I was distraught at being alone. In one of my fits of anger, I heard this still, small voice say, "You asked for this."

When I heard this, I couldn't help but think, *Yeah, I asked a year ago, not now!* This is when I first realized His timing was not my timing.

Once my life changed and I was attending an in-depth Bible study for about a year, I started listening to the Bible Broadcasting Network Radio (www.bbn.org). I stopped listening to any type of secular music, and my radio dial never switched from BBN. (Back then, BBN was the only Christian station available.) I even listened to BBN all night long while I slept. One night, when I went to bed, all of a sudden, I heard that instrumental music for the first time since the nights of listening to it on that cassette. I sat straight up in bed and turned the light on, waiting for them to give the name of the music. I couldn't believe I was hearing the music again that made me feel so peaceful and content. They never gave the name of the music.

I called the radio station on several occasions, trying to get the name but to no avail. I explained how important this music was to me. I would listen every night just to hear that music. Not long after that, they actually played the music during the day, and it had words. It was *My Peace I Give unto You* (http://www.youtube.com/watch?v=nLm-gm2HLwo). The words to the music are so simple and pure as shown in the first verse below:

> My peace I give unto you
> It's a peace that the world cannot give
> It's a peace that the world cannot understand
> Peace to know, peace to live,
> My peace I give unto you.

That night, His still, small voice impressed upon me that He was calling to me ever since that day back in 1987. He was preparing me to receive Him. He does reveal Himself to us, but we have to be receptive. We need to know only He can provide that peace and contentment we desire and long to have. We can know without question He does hear us when we cry out to Him, and He is faithful and true. I'm so full of His love for me that I sometimes uncontrollably sob to think He chose me to be saved from an eternity without Him. Take comfort in knowing He will and can do the same for you. All you have to do is ask, and He will be faithful to answer.

> God is faithful, who has called you into fellowship with his Son, Jesus Christ our Lord (1 Corinthians 1:9).

> Ask and it will be given to you; seek and you will find; knock and the door will be opened to you (Matthew 7:7).

WHEN GOD SPEAKS, LISTEN!

I was thinking about buying a piece of land. A friend of mine telephoned me about an upcoming sale of three acres down the road from where I lived. My friend gave me the name of the guy to contact, and I called him. He promised his land that he would call and give me the first option when he got ready to sell. I was so excited!

I really prayed about buying this land. I asked Jesus to let me know whether I should buy it or not. For several nights, I prayed about this decision because I didn't have that peace I so desperately sought. I drove by the property and thought to myself how pretty it was, but every time I got home, the thought of "It's narrow" would go through my mind. I couldn't figure out for the life of me why I kept thinking, "It's narrow." This process occurred several times. I even told a couple of my friends about this and how I wondered why I kept thinking "It's narrow" when I knew it wasn't. I also took one of my girlfriends over to see the property, and she had no idea why I kept hearing that it was narrow because it wasn't at all narrow.

I finally realized if I was having this much trouble finding peace in buying this land, then it couldn't be the right decision. As soon as I came to this conclusion, my telephone rang. It was the guy with the land for sale. He called to tell me he was ready to negotiate. He had two wells and two septic tanks already on his property, and my friend told me he used to rent out one of the spaces. I asked the guy why he stopped renting the space, and he told me that he had sold a part of his land. I said, "I thought you had three acres."

He said, "I did at one time, but I sold half of it. Now the portion I have left leaves me with a road frontage that's really narrow."

Was this a coincidence? I don't think so!

Sometimes we pray and ask the Lord to direct us, and when He does, we don't really hear Him. It puts me in awe to know He was speaking to me all along, and it makes me realize that when I pray, I must expect Him to answer!

> Jesus replied, "I tell you the truth, if you have faith and do not doubt, not only can you do what was done to the fig tree, but also you can say to this mountain, 'Go, throw yourself into the sea,' and it will be done. If you believe, you will receive whatever you ask for in prayer" (Matthew 21:21–22).

GOD REALLY
DOES ANSWER

I bought a mobile home ten years ago after going through a "homeless" period in my life. The Lord really supplied my needs, even though it was hard for me to see His intervention at the time. He brought people into my life who allowed me to stay with them until I could get on my feet and purchase my first home. I can remember standing in the middle of my living room praising the Lord and thanking Him for such a beautiful mobile home. I was so humbled and thankful to have a place to call mine.

I've served the Lord with all my heart throughout the ten years of living in this home. I've also continued to sing and speak anywhere He opened the door for me to glorify His name. I've had a good life in this mobile home up until about four years ago when I felt led by the Holy Spirit to buy a stick-built house. I started looking for a house but never found anything I really wanted. After a while, I stopped looking.

I remember seeing one house in particular with a For Sale sign in the yard and telling the Lord I would love to have a house like that one. I knew I'd probably never be able to afford to buy a house that nice. Each year over the past three years, I've occasionally gone on a house search. This is the fourth year, and it's been no different. I told my coworkers I really felt an urgency to buy a stick-built house, but I didn't really know why. I told them I was seriously looking on and off over the past few months, but I hadn't found anything I wanted to buy yet.

One day I found a little house I started to settle for, but I couldn't seem to get peace about making an offer to the seller. I wanted a garage and something a little bigger. This house was only 150 square feet larger than my mobile home, and it had no garage. After my third trip to look it over, I realized it wasn't the house for me.

As I pulled out of the driveway and headed down the road, I cried out to the Lord, saying, "Do you really want me to have a house? I can't find one, and I don't know what to do. Please help me!" I was crying and pleading for Him to tell me what to do. All of a sudden, I came around this little curve, and there sat the most beautiful home I ever saw with a For Sale sign in the yard.

I pulled up in front of the house and took one of those little information sheets out of the box but said, "Lord, I can't afford this house."

In my spirit, I heard this still, small, voice say, "You never offer what they're asking."

I called a friend of mine who was a realtor, and she made an appointment for me to go in and look at the house. I couldn't believe it! It was exactly what I dreamed of plus a whole lot more! Not only did it have a garage built on the end of the house, but it also had a detached three-car garage with a wired workshop to boot.

The owner and I went back and forth on a price, and they finally accepted my offer. I couldn't believe it! We set the closing date. The time approached for me to sign on the dotted line, and I started to get cold feet. It was nine days before I was supposed to close the deal. I stood in my mobile home and cried out to the Lord. I said, "Lord, please let me know that you really want me to buy this house!" I told Him that I'd be perfectly content to stay in my mobile home where I felt safe and it was paid for in full. I told Him if it wasn't His will for me to buy this house, then please . . . please shut the door!

The next morning, I got up, went to work, and told my coworkers about what I asked the Lord to do the night before. I also shared with them how I was just going to trust that His will would be done in the situation.

When I arrived home after work that day, a neighbor informed me that the owner of the land where forty-one other families and I lived was selling it to a developer to build homes in the $300,000 price range. I got in my truck and drove up the road to the landowner's house to ask about this rumor, and it was true. I felt so blessed! God clearly showed me His will for me and my new home. I then proceeded with the closing of the house.

After the closing, I pulled into the driveway of my new home. I stopped and sat for a moment, taking in its beauty, when, all of a sudden, the Lord brought to my memory that this was the same house I'd seen four years before with another For Sale sign in the yard! I couldn't believe this! I called the old owner from my vehicle, and she told me they purchased the house four years before from the builder who lived there for five years. How perfect is my God who heard me four years ago regarding this house! He gave me the desire of my heart. I am forever humbled by His love and favor toward me.

I now tell others about the wonderful love and guidance that come from my Lord and Savior Jesus Christ. He is such an awesome God! He is my best friend. I trust Him like no other, and I will praise Him throughout eternity. I was saved again from being homeless, but now I needed to sell a mobile home no one wanted because it had to be moved because of the developer's plan to build new homes on the land. The person who bought my mobile home would need to own land and be able to move the home to its new location. I placed ads in newspapers, put a For Sale sign on the home, and told everyone I knew, even people I didn't know. I had no success selling the home.

I got down on my knees and cried out to Jesus again. I pleaded with Him to send someone to buy my mobile home and appreciate it as much as I did. I told Him I didn't know what else to do to sell it, and I needed Him to take care of it for me.

The next morning, I got up, went to work, and told my coworkers about what I asked the Lord the night before. When I returned home that evening, I didn't even think about checking my voicemail until about eight. When I picked up my phone, I heard this lady's voicemail message saying that she and her husband drove by my mobile home and were very interested in seeing it. I called her, and they met me at the mobile home.

Are you ready for this? They made an offer. The mobile home was sold! I met her at the mobile home a day or so later so she could take some measurements in the house. As I was emptying the remaining frozen food from my freezer to take to my new house, I overheard her speaking with great enthusiasm to her husband. I turned around and saw her standing in the middle of the floor, exclaiming how she could just stand there and look around at this mobile home all day long! She said this was the nicest home that they ever owned.

As tears rolled down my face, she was so sweet, wanting to know if I was all right. I told her that she just stated the very words I said when I stood in that very spot on the first day I moved into the mobile home. She assured me that they would take really good care of my home.

At that moment, I felt the Lord wrap His arms around me. God provided and led me to a new home as an answer to prayer. He also found new owners for my old home who would treasure it and appreciate it as much as I did. God answered all my prayers in His perfect timing and in His perfect ways. Oh, how I love my Father in heaven, who is so good to me, a sinner saved by His marvelous grace! Amen and amen.

Lesson learned:

> The LORD is a refuge for the oppressed, a stronghold in times of trouble. Those who know Your name will trust in You, for You, LORD, have never forsaken those who seek You. Sing praises to the LORD, enthroned in Zion; proclaim among the nations what He has done (Psalm 9:9–11).

REJOICE IN THE LORD ALWAYS

I accepted the responsibility of keeping the bulletin board displayed as you entered the church. I didn't get to create the bulletin board for September until the Saturday evening before the Sunday-morning service. After seeking instruction from my Lord, I was searching the internet, which led me to a site where the lead sheet music for a song entitled "I Will Rejoice" popped up. The words to this song were really nice, and the following scripture came to mind:

> "Rejoice in the Lord always. I will say it again rejoice!" (Philippians 4:4).

Since the sheet music was free for download, I decided to print and utilize it in creating the bulletin board, along with the scripture.

I tell you that for some months there, I felt as though my Lord wasn't hearing me. He was not near me. I was feeling like I didn't belong anywhere, and that included the church where I was planted. For some time, I felt like an outcast. It seemed my world was crumbling around me bit by bit. It was difficult to keep up with my home. I sought my Lord, requesting His help; but so far, there wasn't much help or answers.

I just continued to struggle from day to day in uncertainty. I couldn't help but wonder if my Lord was angry with me because of His silence. Sunday morning came, and I wasn't planning on going to church. I was tired and washed out from working all week, singing at a revival on Friday night, and doing chores all day Saturday. But around 9:30 a.m., I decided to go. I arrived at church, picked up my bulletin, and sat down.

The service began as the choir stood up to sing the call to worship. They started singing a song titled "Rejoice in the Lord Always." As they finished singing, the pastor stood up and started to read Philippians 4:4. I felt a wave of emotion come over me while tears started to fill my eyes. I felt as if my Lord was wrapping His arms around me.

As soon as these feelings and thoughts enveloped me, I started to hear in my spirit that the choir director must have seen the bulletin board this morning when she arrived, which made her choose this particular song for the call to worship. Also, she must have coordinated with the pastor on the scripture he would use at the morning service. Most of all, it had absolutely *nothing* to do with the Lord speaking to me. The logical side of me accepted these thoughts as truth, and I thought no more about the issue.

Later in the evening, I called the lady who was in charge of some new programs that were coming up at church, and I wanted to discuss some of them with her. While talking to her, I asked if she saw the bulletin board that morning. One thing led to another, and I was telling her about the call-to-worship song and how they must have seen the bulletin board and decided to sing "Rejoice in the Lord Always." She said she thought the bulletins were printed ahead of time.

I jumped up and looked at my bulletin. "Rejoice in the Lord Always" was shown as the call to worship, and the scripture the pastor read was outlined right there in black and white. I hung up, called the music director, and asked her if she noticed the bulletin board that morning. She said yes. She said as soon as I walked in, she couldn't help but think how cool it was the way God orchestrates things! I said, "So you didn't see the bulletin board until Sunday morning?"

She said no, she hadn't. She said she didn't even choose the song for the call to worship until late Saturday night. She and her husband were moving all day, and she wasn't sure if she could get it in the bulletin because she waited so late to call the lady who prints our bulletins.

To say the least, I had a knot in my throat so big I could hardly speak, and the tears started to flow from my eyes. I don't know why I'm always so surprised when Jesus communicates His Love to me. He has never forsaken me. Why I feel like He has sometimes, I'll never fully understand. My only guess is that I desire to have constant communication with Him, and when He's quiet, I feel alone! I guess I'm like that child who's always craving attention from their parents and feels abandoned when the attention isn't constantly evident. I also believe this is a perfect example of the Lord displaying His love, mercy, and grace and how Satan attempts to steal. Never forget that we must

> Rejoice in the Lord Always. I say it again rejoice! (Philippians 4:4).

> Keep your lives free from the love of money and be content with what you have, because God has said, "Never will I leave you; never will I forsake you" (Hebrews 13:5).

GOD WILL PROVIDE

Here I was, living in this beautiful home for the past four and a half years when I felt compelled to sell my home. It was getting harder and harder to maintain this home alone. I even reached the point of not being able to make my house payment. I knew this was an awful time to try to sell my home because the bottom just dropped out of the housing market. Even my neighbor who lived behind me was trying to sell their home for the past four years, and they were just now in the process of closing on their home. I became very distraught. I pleaded with Jesus to help me because I didn't know what to do.

While waiting on the Lord, I continued to sell off my belongings to continue paying what bills I could. I managed to catch up on everything but one payment on my home. I was struggling and still pleading with Jesus to help me.

One day during the week, I was coming down with an extremely bad cold when my phone rang. It was my neighbors who used to live behind me. They wanted to drop by and see me as they were in the neighborhood tying up some loose ends. I told them I'd love for them to come by, but I didn't want them to catch my terrible cold. The wife told me they just wanted to drop by and give me something but they wouldn't come inside. I had no idea what they wanted to give me. As she approached the front door, she reached for the door handle and slipped an envelope inside. She said that she and her husband wanted me to have this, and they wanted me to know that it was a gift. They waved at me as they drove away. I took the envelope, and when I opened it, I fell apart.

Tears of joy, humility, and thanksgiving filled my heart as I dropped to my knees in praise of Jesus. It was fifteen $100 bills for my house payment. No one can tell me Jesus doesn't hear prayers!

Later that week, I knew without a doubt I needed to put my house on the market. I prayed and asked Jesus to send the right couple to buy my house. It just went on the market, and a young couple from Winston-Salem, North Carolina, made an offer the morning after they saw the house. I felt an urgency to go ahead and let the house go without making one dime. It was impressed upon me that I just needed to get out from under the mortgage. So that's exactly what I did. Boy, was I glad I listened to the Holy Spirit because six months after I moved, I was laid off from my job after thirteen years of service. Praise Jesus! If I hadn't listened, I would've really lost everything, and I might have never experienced what Jesus had waiting for me around the bend.

Jesus taught me several lessons that year. Just because He allows us to have something we've always desired such as a beautiful home, it doesn't always mean we're meant to permanently keep it. Just because our lives change and we have to do something like move away from our comfort zone and make a new start without knowing anyone, it doesn't mean our life is over. In fact, as in my case, it was a new beginning that led to the fulfillment of another desire of my heart.

> That is why I tell you not to worry about everyday life—whether you have enough food and drink, or enough clothes to wear. Isn't life more than food, and your body more than clothing? Look at the birds. They don't plant or harvest or store food in barns, for your heavenly Father feeds them. And aren't you far more valuable to him than they are? Can all your worries add a single moment to your life? (Matthew 6:26–27).

TOTALED VEHICLE

I totaled my car on February 6, 2020. I was taken to the hospital and ended up in room 33. I couldn't help but think about Jesus dying for my sins and saving me when He was thirty-three years old; now, here I lay in room 33, and He has saved me again.

After leaving the hospital, I contacted my insurance company the next day and was given my claim number, which began with 33. I called the lady for the payoff information of my totaled Abarth by Fiat and had to leave her a message on her extension number 333.

After recuperating for a little over ten days, I started my search for another vehicle. I bought my last two vehicles from Hendrick's, so I decided to look there. I met this nice young man named Vincent who was truly a delight! We talked for a while, and I began to talk to him about the Lord. He was so receptive. He shared his story with me, and we instantly realized we had a lot in common. He had a really bad accident some time ago, and it was touch-and-go for a while. He truly believed God was with him as everywhere he went after being released from the hospital, he saw hearts. He had an abundance of pictures of hearts on his phone, and his pictures were amazing as he really had eyes to see that God was with him all the time. I gave him one of my Heart of Jesus Ministries cards, and he asked if he could keep it. Of course, I said absolutely!

He was helping me search for the vehicle I thought I wanted. We had talked for a while, and he told me he thought he understood exactly what I was looking for; and sure enough, he did, even though I had *never ever* wanted this kind of car. But when I saw it, I really liked it for some reason. I told him I would like to test-drive it, and so he darted out the door to bring the car over for me to test-drive. When he returned, I started taking pictures of the car. I thought it was a cool-looking vehicle.

Before we started our test-drive, he said, "I have something to share with you that just came to my mind." I was eager to hear what he wanted to tell me. He said, "You aren't going to believe this." By now, I was really intrigued. He proceeded to take his driver's license out of his wallet (which he allowed me to take a picture of) and showed it to me. I didn't get it at first when he said, "I had a birthday a few days ago." His birthday was February 13, 1987. He had just turned thirty-three years old!

I had Holy Spirit bumps come all over me. Needless to say, I bought this car. It drives and rides great. I purchased a 2018 Kia Soul with only nine thousand miles on it. One owner with no accidents. Fully loaded. Thank you, Jesus! I am truly blessed, and I give all praise and glory to my Lord and Savior Christ Jesus.

HE SAVED THE
BEST FOR LAST

I t was late December. I just sold my house and was moving some thirty miles away to be closer to work. I knew the first thing I wanted to do was find a new church home, so I got busy on the internet. I started by locating all the churches close to my new home. I made a list and started mapping out directions to start attending one new church every week. I visited church after church, never feeling the Holy Spirit at any of them. I was very discouraged. I asked Jesus to lead me to a church where I felt like I belonged. I wanted a sense of family, as my immediate family had gone on into eternity. I really wanted to feel like I belonged somewhere and not just visiting.

Many weeks later, I came to the last church on my list. I awoke that Sunday morning and told the Lord that I wouldn't go to church and save the last church for next Sunday. I watched *Turning Point* with Dr. David Jeremiah, and after that, I told the Lord I would go ahead and go to church.

Upon arrival, I entered the church. As soon as I stepped into the foyer, I felt the strong presence of the Holy Spirit. I hadn't felt that in a mighty long time. I was so captivated I continued on into the sanctuary. The next thing I knew, I was halfway down the aisle. I couldn't believe it because in every church prior to this one, I immediately sat in the back pew. I stepped into the center pew and sat down when a lady sitting in front of me turned around and introduced herself. We immediately hit it off. She said she'd been praying that the Lord would send her a godly friend, as her best friend died a few weeks before, and she really missed her.

She said, "Ellen, I don't believe it's a coincidence that you came and sat down behind me this morning." We both agreed that there are no coincidences with Jesus. The service began.

I enjoyed myself tremendously! After the service, my new friend asked if she could give me a hug. I said, "Of course!" Hugs are always good, especially when you live alone. She told me she really hoped I'd come back. I told her I most definitely would. I didn't know why, but I felt that I was supposed to be at this church. As I waited in line to shake the pastor's hand, I was filled with excitement in knowing I found a church where the Holy Spirit lived.

When I reached the pastor, he extended his hand to welcome me. It all happened so quickly. He said, "So glad to have you here this morning. What's your name?"

I said "Ellen Harlow."

He said, "Is that Harlow [spelled out my last name]?"

I said, "Yes."

He said, "Wouldn't happen to be a kin of the Harlows up in the northern part of the state around Halifax County, would you?"

I know I must have looked perplexed as I said, "Well, yes, as a matter of fact, that is where I was born and raised."

He said, "Who's your mama and daddy?"

I said, "Louise and Alvin Harlow."

He then said, "Oh my goodness, was your brother Ricky Harlow?" At that moment, my mouth flew wide open in awe, and I couldn't control the tears that began to fall from my eyes. He said, "I'm Pastor Phil Qualls." He said, "Your brother and I were best friends growing up. We played sports together. Your mama has fixed me many a cheeseburger and french fries. I've spent the night in your house many times when you were just a little girl."

By this time, the tears had taken me over. Pastor Phil was ten years older than me, so I was about seven years old when I first met him. I remembered the face of the teenage boy, but I would've never known the man he'd become. Needless to say, I walked out of that church that morning in a pure stupor. Wet face and all.

I'm now a member of this church, and I'm so thankful to my Lord and Savior for answering my prayer. I'm so glad I didn't stay home that morning. If I gave in to my flesh, look at the blessing I would've missed! Pastor Phil and I have spent many moments reminiscing about the past. I now have a wonderful church family that I'm growing to love more and more every day!

I feel that my Lord has brought me full circle. Coincidence? Absolutely *not*! Not only did He answer my prayer and give me a wonderful church family, but He also gave me a pastor who knew me when I was a child. I humbly praise and thank you, my Lord, for hearing and answering my prayer! All the while, He was saving the best for last! How precious is that?

> Trust in the LORD and do good; dwell in the land
> and enjoy safe pasture. Take delight in the LORD,
> and He will give you the desires of your heart.
> Commit your way to the LORD; trust in Him and
> He will do this (Psalm 37:3–5).

DETAILED SCRIPTURE REFERENCES TO HOMOSEXUALITY

Leviticus 20:22

"Keep all my decrees and laws and follow them, so that the land where I am bringing you to live may not vomit you out."

Genesis 19:1–8

"The two angels arrived at Sodom in the evening, and Lot was sitting in the gateway of the city. When he saw them, he got up to meet them and bowed down with his face to the ground. 'My lords,' he said, 'please turn aside to your servant's house. You can wash your feet and spend the night and then go on your way early in the morning.' 'No,' they answered, 'we will spend the night in the square.' But he insisted so strongly that they did go with him and entered his house. He prepared a meal for them, baking bread without yeast, and they ate. Before they had gone to bed, all the men from every part of the city of Sodom—both young and old—surrounded the house. They called to Lot, 'Where are the men who came to you tonight? Bring them out to us so that we can have sex with them.' Lot went outside to meet them and shut the door behind him and said, 'No, my friends. Don't do this wicked thing. Look, I have two daughters who have never slept with a man. Let me bring them out to you, and you can do what you like with them. But don't do anything to these men, for they have come under the protection of my roof.'"

Judges 19:22–23

"While they were enjoying themselves, some of the wicked men of the city surrounded the house. Pounding on the door, they shouted to the old man who owned the house, 'Bring out the man who came to your house so we can have sex with him.' The owner of the house went outside and said to them, 'No, my friends, don't be so vile. Since this man is my guest, don't do this disgraceful thing.'"

Romans 1:24–27

"Therefore God gave them over in the sinful desires of their hearts to sexual impurity for the degrading of their bodies with one another. They exchanged the truth of God for a lie, and worshiped and served created things rather than the Creator—who is forever praised. Amen. Because of this, God gave them over to shameful lusts. Even their women exchanged natural relations for unnatural ones. In the same way the men also abandoned natural relations with women and were inflamed with lust for one another. Men committed indecent acts with other men, and received in themselves the due penalty for their perversion."

1 Corinthians 6:9–10

"Do you not know that the wicked will not inherit the kingdom of God? Do not be deceived: Neither the sexually immoral nor idolaters nor adulterers nor male prostitutes nor homosexual offenders nor thieves nor the greedy nor drunkards nor slanderers nor swindlers will inherit the kingdom of God."

**Leviticus 18:22

"Do not lie with a man as one lies with a woman; that is detestable."

**Leviticus 20:13

"If a man lies with a man as one lies with a woman, both of them have done what is detestable. They must be put to death; their blood will be on their own heads."

Meaning

**The first *lie* in the sentence literally means to just lie down and can mean anybody simply physically lying beside another person. The kicker is, the term *as with womankind* also means "to lay" but has the clear meaning of carnal intercourse.

So it's clear that the Old Testament forbids a man to lay with another man for carnal intercourse.

How about the question of the Bible actually speaking about homosexuality? The answer to this lies in the fact that the Greek word is actually a combination of two other Greek words whose *new* meaning after the combination is clearly the description of homosexual activity. The scripture reference in the Greek *arsenokoites* comes from the joining of two other Greek words:

1. *arrhen* (ar'-hrane) or *arsen* (ar'-sane)—male (as stronger for lifting), which simply means male or man.
2. *koite* (koy'-tay)—a couch; by extension, cohabitation; by implication, the male sperm and is translated on its own to mean "bed," "chambering," and "to conceive."

All the New Testament references to *bed* are listed above for you to see or look up. It's interesting, though, that the word *koite* is used three out of the four times to mean a sexual reference to the bed all by itself.

Also—this is interesting—we get the English word *coitus* (pronounced *koy-tus*), which means the actual act of intercourse. The combination of these two Greek words is unique in their description of the homosexual based on his activity. There is no question about this. So as you can see, the Greek word for what a homosexual would do is quite clear, although there's no actual label for the person. However, the word *clearly* means a man who lies with another man for the purpose of having a sexual relationship not only by definition but also by context and implication. Everyone has a choice. God's Word is clear on that, so will you choose to follow Jesus and his commands or your own lustful sinful ways?

> If you declare with your mouth, "Jesus is Lord," and believe in your heart that God raised him from the dead, you will be saved. For it is with your heart that you believe and are justified, and it is with your mouth that you profess your faith and are saved. As Scripture says, "Anyone who believes in him will never be put to shame." For there is no difference between Jew and Gentile—the same Lord is Lord of all and richly blesses all who call on him, for, "Everyone who calls on the name of the Lord will be saved."

WAKE UP, CHURCH!

Printed in the United States
by Baker & Taylor Publisher Services